50 Slow-Cooked Perfection Recipes

By: Kelly Johnson

Table of Contents

- Beef Stew
- Pulled Pork
- Chicken Tikka Masala
- BBQ Ribs
- Slow-Cooked Chili
- Pot Roast
- Beef Brisket
- Chicken and Dumplings
- Vegetable Soup
- Baked Ziti
- Meatballs in Marinara Sauce
- Sweet and Sour Chicken
- Slow-Cooked Beef Bourguignon
- Honey Garlic Chicken
- French Onion Soup
- Slow-Cooked Lamb Shanks
- Chicken Alfredo

- Slow-Cooked Beef Chili
- Baked Beans
- Pork Carnitas
- Slow-Cooked Ratatouille
- Chicken Fajitas
- Creamy Chicken and Rice
- Slow-Cooked Corned Beef and Cabbage
- Chicken Parmesan
- Vegetable Curry
- Slow-Cooked Barbacoa Beef
- Mushroom Stroganoff
- Chicken Enchiladas
- Slow-Cooked Stuffed Peppers
- Creamy White Chicken Chili
- Slow-Cooked Sausage and Peppers
- Pork Roast with Apples and Carrots
- Beef and Potato Stew
- Chicken Marsala
- Slow-Cooked Jambalaya

- Thai Red Curry Chicken

- Slow-Cooked Shepherd's Pie

- Beef and Vegetable Soup

- Slow-Cooked Meatloaf

- Chicken and Wild Rice Soup

- Slow-Cooked Baked Ziti

- Braised Short Ribs

- Chicken Tortilla Soup

- Slow-Cooked Goulash

- Turkey Chili

- Slow-Cooked Sausage and Lentils

- Sweet Potato and Black Bean Stew

- Slow-Cooked Apple Cinnamon Oatmeal

- Beef and Bean Burritos

Beef Stew

Ingredients:

- 2 lbs beef chuck, cut into 1-inch cubes
- Salt & pepper
- 2 tbsp flour
- 2 tbsp olive oil
- 1 onion, chopped
- 3 cloves garlic, minced
- 3 cups beef broth
- 1 cup red wine (optional)
- 2 tbsp tomato paste
- 1 tsp thyme
- 1 tsp rosemary
- 3 carrots, chopped
- 3 potatoes, peeled and cubed
- 2 celery stalks, chopped

Instructions:

1. Season beef with salt and pepper, toss with flour.
2. In a large pot, heat oil over medium-high heat and brown the beef in batches.

3. Add onions and garlic, cook until soft.

4. Stir in broth, wine, tomato paste, and herbs.

5. Add the browned beef back, bring to a simmer.

6. Cover and simmer for 1.5–2 hours, then add vegetables.

7. Cook for another 45 minutes until veggies are tender.

Pulled Pork

Ingredients:

- 3–4 lb pork shoulder
- 1 tbsp paprika
- 1 tbsp brown sugar
- 1 tsp garlic powder
- 1 tsp onion powder
- 1 tsp salt
- 1/2 tsp pepper
- 1 cup BBQ sauce
- 1/2 cup apple cider vinegar
- 1/2 cup chicken broth

Instructions:

1. Mix all dry spices and rub over pork.
2. Place pork in slow cooker. Pour vinegar and broth over.
3. Cook on low for 8 hours or high for 5 hours.
4. Shred with forks, mix in BBQ sauce.
5. Serve on buns, tacos, or over rice.

Chicken Tikka Masala

Ingredients:

- 1 lb chicken breast or thighs, cubed
- 1 cup plain yogurt
- 1 tbsp lemon juice
- 2 tsp garam masala
- 1 tsp turmeric
- 1 tsp paprika
- 2 tsp ground cumin
- Salt

For the sauce:

- 1 onion, diced
- 3 garlic cloves, minced
- 1 tbsp grated ginger
- 1 can (15 oz) tomato sauce
- 1 cup heavy cream
- 2 tbsp butter
- Cilantro, for garnish

Instructions:

1. Marinate chicken in yogurt, lemon juice, and spices for at least 1 hour.

2. Cook chicken in skillet until browned. Set aside.

3. Sauté onions, garlic, and ginger until soft.

4. Add tomato sauce and simmer 10 minutes.

5. Add cream and butter, return chicken to pan.

6. Simmer until thickened. Garnish with cilantro.

BBQ Ribs

Ingredients:

- 2 racks baby back ribs
- 1/4 cup brown sugar
- 2 tsp paprika
- 1 tsp garlic powder
- 1 tsp onion powder
- Salt and pepper
- 1–2 cups BBQ sauce

Instructions:

1. Preheat oven to 300°F (150°C).
2. Mix spices and rub onto ribs. Wrap in foil.
3. Bake ribs for 2.5–3 hours until tender.
4. Unwrap and brush with BBQ sauce.
5. Broil or grill for 5–10 minutes to caramelize.

Slow-Cooked Chili

Ingredients:

- 1 lb ground beef
- 1 onion, diced
- 3 cloves garlic, minced
- 1 can diced tomatoes
- 1 can kidney beans
- 1 can black beans
- 2 tbsp chili powder
- 1 tsp cumin
- 1 tsp smoked paprika
- Salt and pepper
- Optional: jalapeño, cheddar, sour cream

Instructions:

1. Brown beef with onion and garlic. Drain fat.
2. Transfer to slow cooker with all other ingredients.
3. Cook on low for 6–8 hours or high for 3–4 hours.
4. Serve with toppings of choice.

Pot Roast

Ingredients:

- 3–4 lb chuck roast
- Salt & pepper
- 2 tbsp oil
- 1 onion, chopped
- 4 cloves garlic
- 2 cups beef broth
- 1 cup red wine (optional)
- 1 tbsp Worcestershire sauce
- 4 carrots, chopped
- 3 potatoes, cubed

Instructions:

1. Season and sear roast in oil on all sides.
2. Sauté onion and garlic, add broth, wine, Worcestershire.
3. Add roast and veggies to slow cooker.
4. Cook on low for 8 hours or until tender.

Beef Brisket

Ingredients:

- 4 lb beef brisket
- 1 tbsp paprika
- 1 tsp garlic powder
- 1 tsp onion powder
- 1 tsp salt
- 1/2 tsp black pepper
- 1 cup beef broth
- 1 cup BBQ sauce

Instructions:

1. Rub brisket with seasoning mix.
2. Place in slow cooker with broth and BBQ sauce.
3. Cook on low 8–10 hours.
4. Slice and serve with extra sauce.

Chicken and Dumplings

Ingredients:

- 1 lb chicken thighs or breasts
- 1 onion, diced
- 2 carrots, sliced
- 2 celery stalks, sliced
- 4 cups chicken broth
- 1 cup frozen peas
- 1 cup heavy cream
- 2 cups biscuit mix
- 2/3 cup milk

Instructions:

1. Sauté onion, carrots, and celery.
2. Add chicken and broth, simmer until cooked through.
3. Shred chicken and return to pot with peas and cream.
4. Mix biscuit mix and milk. Drop spoonfuls into soup.
5. Cover and simmer 15 minutes until dumplings are cooked.

Vegetable Soup

Ingredients:

- 1 tbsp olive oil
- 1 onion, chopped
- 2 garlic cloves
- 3 carrots, sliced
- 2 celery stalks
- 1 zucchini, diced
- 1 can diced tomatoes
- 4 cups vegetable broth
- 1 tsp Italian seasoning
- Salt & pepper
- 1 cup green beans or peas

Instructions:

1. Sauté onion, garlic, carrots, and celery.
2. Add remaining ingredients and bring to boil.
3. Simmer 25–30 minutes until veggies are tender.
4. Adjust seasoning and serve.

Baked Ziti

Ingredients:

- 1 lb ziti pasta
- 1 lb ground beef or sausage
- 1 jar (24 oz) marinara sauce
- 1 cup ricotta cheese
- 1 egg
- 2 cups shredded mozzarella
- 1/4 cup grated Parmesan

Instructions:

1. Cook pasta until al dente.
2. Brown meat and add marinara.
3. Mix ricotta, egg, salt, and pepper.
4. In a baking dish, layer pasta, ricotta, meat sauce, mozzarella.
5. Repeat and top with Parmesan.
6. Bake at 375°F (190°C) for 30–35 minutes until bubbly.

Meatballs in Marinara Sauce

Ingredients:

- 1 lb ground beef
- 1/2 cup breadcrumbs
- 1/4 cup grated Parmesan
- 1 egg
- 2 cloves garlic, minced
- 1 tsp Italian seasoning
- Salt & pepper
- 2 cups marinara sauce
- Fresh basil (optional)

Instructions:

1. Mix beef, breadcrumbs, Parmesan, egg, garlic, and seasoning.
2. Form into 1-inch balls.
3. Brown in a skillet or bake at 400°F (200°C) for 15 minutes.
4. Simmer in marinara sauce for 20 minutes.
5. Serve over pasta or in subs.

Sweet and Sour Chicken

Ingredients:

- 1 lb chicken breast, cubed
- 1/2 cup cornstarch
- 2 eggs, beaten
- Oil for frying

Sauce:

- 1/2 cup sugar
- 1/4 cup ketchup
- 1/2 cup vinegar
- 1 tbsp soy sauce
- 1 tsp garlic powder

Instructions:

1. Coat chicken in cornstarch, then dip in egg.
2. Fry until golden and drain on paper towels.
3. Mix sauce ingredients, pour over chicken.
4. Bake at 350°F (175°C) for 25 minutes, stirring halfway.

Slow-Cooked Beef Bourguignon

Ingredients:

- 2.5 lbs beef chuck, cubed
- 6 oz bacon, chopped
- 2 carrots, chopped
- 1 onion, diced
- 3 garlic cloves
- 2 tbsp tomato paste
- 2 cups red wine
- 2 cups beef broth
- 1 tsp thyme
- 1 bay leaf
- 1 tbsp flour
- 1 cup mushrooms

Instructions:

1. Brown bacon, then remove.
2. Brown beef in bacon fat.
3. Sauté vegetables, add tomato paste, then flour.
4. Add wine, broth, herbs, and beef.

5. Cook on low for 8 hours.

6. Add mushrooms in last hour. Serve with mashed potatoes or bread.

Honey Garlic Chicken

Ingredients:

- 1.5 lbs chicken thighs
- Salt & pepper
- 1/2 cup honey
- 1/4 cup soy sauce
- 4 garlic cloves, minced
- 1 tbsp rice vinegar
- 1 tbsp cornstarch + 2 tbsp water (optional, for thickening)

Instructions:

1. Season chicken and brown both sides in a skillet.
2. Whisk honey, soy sauce, garlic, vinegar.
3. Pour over chicken and simmer 20–25 minutes.
4. Thicken sauce if desired. Serve over rice.

French Onion Soup

Ingredients:

- 4 large onions, sliced
- 3 tbsp butter
- 2 tbsp flour
- 1/2 cup dry white wine (optional)
- 6 cups beef broth
- 1 tsp thyme
- Baguette slices
- Gruyère or mozzarella cheese

Instructions:

1. Caramelize onions in butter over low heat (about 30 mins).
2. Stir in flour, cook 2 mins, then add wine.
3. Add broth and thyme, simmer 30 mins.
4. Ladle into bowls, top with toast and cheese.
5. Broil until bubbly.

Slow-Cooked Lamb Shanks

Ingredients:

- 4 lamb shanks
- Salt & pepper
- 2 tbsp olive oil
- 1 onion, chopped
- 3 garlic cloves
- 2 carrots, chopped
- 1 cup red wine
- 2 cups beef broth
- 1 tbsp tomato paste
- 1 tsp rosemary
- 1 bay leaf

Instructions:

1. Brown shanks in oil, set aside.
2. Sauté onion, garlic, and carrots.
3. Add wine, broth, tomato paste, and herbs.
4. Place everything in slow cooker. Cook on low for 8 hours.
5. Serve with mashed potatoes or polenta.

Chicken Alfredo

Ingredients:

- 2 chicken breasts, sliced
- 2 tbsp butter
- 2 cups heavy cream
- 1 cup Parmesan cheese
- 2 cloves garlic, minced
- 1 lb fettuccine
- Salt & pepper

Instructions:

1. Cook pasta and drain.
2. Cook chicken in skillet and set aside.
3. Melt butter, add garlic, then cream.
4. Simmer 5 minutes, stir in cheese until melted.
5. Add pasta and chicken, toss to coat.

Slow-Cooked Beef Chili

Ingredients:

- 1 lb ground beef
- 1 onion, chopped
- 1 bell pepper, chopped
- 2 garlic cloves
- 2 cans diced tomatoes
- 1 can kidney beans
- 1 can black beans
- 2 tbsp chili powder
- 1 tsp cumin
- Salt & pepper

Instructions:

1. Brown beef with onion, pepper, and garlic.
2. Transfer to slow cooker with remaining ingredients.
3. Cook on low 6–8 hours. Serve with cornbread or chips.

Baked Beans

Ingredients:

- 4 cups cooked navy beans
- 1 onion, diced
- 1/2 cup brown sugar
- 1/2 cup ketchup
- 1/4 cup molasses
- 2 tbsp mustard
- 1/2 tsp smoked paprika
- Salt & pepper

Instructions:

1. Preheat oven to 325°F (165°C).
2. Combine all ingredients in a baking dish.
3. Bake covered for 1 hour, then uncovered for 30 mins until thick.

Pork Carnitas

Ingredients:

- 3–4 lb pork shoulder
- 1 tbsp oregano
- 1 tsp cumin
- 1 tbsp chili powder
- Salt & pepper
- 1 onion, chopped
- 4 garlic cloves
- 1/2 cup orange juice
- 1/2 cup lime juice

Instructions:

1. Rub pork with spices, place in slow cooker with juices, onion, garlic.
2. Cook on low 8–10 hours until tender.
3. Shred meat, then broil 5–10 minutes until crispy.
4. Serve in tacos, burritos, or bowls.

Slow-Cooked Ratatouille

Ingredients:

- 1 eggplant, cubed
- 2 zucchinis, sliced
- 1 red bell pepper, chopped
- 1 yellow bell pepper, chopped
- 1 onion, chopped
- 3 cloves garlic, minced
- 1 (14 oz) can crushed tomatoes
- 2 tbsp olive oil
- 1 tsp thyme
- Salt & pepper to taste
- Fresh basil (for garnish)

Instructions:

1. Add all vegetables, garlic, and tomatoes to a slow cooker.
2. Drizzle with olive oil, add thyme, salt, and pepper.
3. Stir gently to combine.
4. Cook on low for 6–8 hours or high for 3–4 hours.
5. Garnish with fresh basil and serve with crusty bread or rice.

Chicken Fajitas

Ingredients:

- 1.5 lbs chicken breasts, sliced
- 1 red bell pepper, sliced
- 1 green bell pepper, sliced
- 1 onion, sliced
- 2 tbsp olive oil
- 2 tsp chili powder
- 1 tsp cumin
- 1/2 tsp paprika
- Salt & pepper
- Tortillas, sour cream, salsa, lime (for serving)

Instructions:

1. In a large bowl, toss chicken, peppers, and onion with oil and seasonings.
2. Sauté in a skillet over medium-high heat for 10–12 minutes until chicken is cooked.
3. Serve in tortillas with toppings of choice.

Creamy Chicken and Rice

Ingredients:

- 1 lb chicken breasts, diced
- 1 cup long-grain rice
- 2 cups chicken broth
- 1 cup milk or cream
- 1/2 cup grated Parmesan
- 1 onion, chopped
- 2 garlic cloves, minced
- 1 cup frozen peas
- Salt, pepper, and thyme

Instructions:

1. In a large skillet, sauté onion and garlic, add chicken and cook until browned.
2. Add rice, broth, and thyme. Bring to a boil.
3. Reduce heat, cover, and simmer 20 minutes.
4. Stir in milk/cream, Parmesan, and peas. Cook 5 more minutes.

Slow-Cooked Corned Beef and Cabbage

Ingredients:

- 3–4 lb corned beef brisket with spice packet
- 4 carrots, chopped
- 1 onion, quartered
- 3 potatoes, chopped
- 1 small cabbage, cut into wedges
- 4 cups water or beef broth

Instructions:

1. Place beef in slow cooker, add carrots, onion, and potatoes.
2. Pour broth over top, sprinkle seasoning packet.
3. Cook on low for 8–9 hours.
4. Add cabbage during the last 2 hours of cooking.
5. Slice and serve hot.

Chicken Parmesan

Ingredients:

- 2 chicken breasts, pounded
- 1/2 cup flour
- 2 eggs, beaten
- 1 cup breadcrumbs
- 1 cup marinara sauce
- 1 cup mozzarella cheese
- 1/2 cup Parmesan cheese
- Salt, pepper, Italian seasoning
- Olive oil for frying

Instructions:

1. Dredge chicken in flour, then egg, then breadcrumbs.
2. Pan-fry until golden and cooked through.
3. Place in a baking dish, top with sauce and cheese.
4. Bake at 400°F (200°C) for 15–20 minutes until bubbly.

Vegetable Curry

Ingredients:

- 2 tbsp oil
- 1 onion, chopped
- 3 garlic cloves, minced
- 1 tbsp curry powder
- 1 tsp turmeric
- 1/2 tsp chili flakes (optional)
- 1 can coconut milk
- 2 cups chopped mixed vegetables (carrot, potato, peas, bell pepper)
- Salt & pepper

Instructions:

1. Sauté onion and garlic in oil. Add curry powder and turmeric.
2. Stir in vegetables and coconut milk.
3. Simmer 20–25 minutes until veggies are tender.
4. Serve with rice or naan.

Slow-Cooked Barbacoa Beef

Ingredients:

- 3–4 lb chuck roast
- 3 chipotle peppers in adobo sauce
- 1/4 cup lime juice
- 4 cloves garlic
- 1 tbsp cumin
- 1 tbsp oregano
- 1/2 tsp ground cloves
- Salt & pepper
- 1/2 cup beef broth

Instructions:

1. Blend chipotles, lime juice, garlic, and seasonings.
2. Place beef in slow cooker and cover with sauce and broth.
3. Cook on low 8–10 hours until tender.
4. Shred and serve in tacos or bowls.

Mushroom Stroganoff

Ingredients:

- 1 tbsp butter
- 1 tbsp olive oil
- 1 onion, chopped
- 2 garlic cloves, minced
- 1 lb mushrooms, sliced
- 1/2 cup vegetable broth
- 1 cup sour cream
- 1 tbsp flour
- Salt, pepper, and parsley
- Cooked egg noodles

Instructions:

1. Sauté onions and garlic in butter/oil.
2. Add mushrooms, cook until browned.
3. Stir in flour, then broth, and simmer.
4. Remove from heat and stir in sour cream.
5. Season to taste and serve over noodles.

Chicken Enchiladas

Ingredients:

- 2 cups cooked, shredded chicken
- 2 cups enchilada sauce
- 1 cup shredded cheese
- 1/2 cup sour cream
- 1/2 onion, diced
- 6-8 flour tortillas

Instructions:

1. Mix chicken with half the cheese, onion, and some sauce.
2. Roll into tortillas and place in a greased baking dish.
3. Cover with remaining sauce and cheese.
4. Bake at 375°F (190°C) for 20-25 minutes.

Slow-Cooked Stuffed Peppers

Ingredients:

- 4 bell peppers, tops cut and seeds removed
- 1 lb ground beef or turkey
- 1 cup cooked rice
- 1/2 onion, chopped
- 1 cup tomato sauce
- 1 tsp Italian seasoning
- 1/2 cup shredded cheese

Instructions:

1. Mix meat, rice, onion, sauce, and seasoning.
2. Stuff mixture into peppers and place in slow cooker.
3. Pour a bit of water or broth around them.
4. Cook on low for 6–7 hours.
5. Top with cheese before serving.

Creamy White Chicken Chili

Ingredients:

- 1 lb boneless skinless chicken breasts
- 1 small onion, chopped
- 2 cloves garlic, minced
- 1 (15 oz) can great northern beans, drained
- 1 (15 oz) can corn, drained
- 1 (4 oz) can diced green chilies
- 1 tsp cumin, 1/2 tsp oregano, 1/2 tsp chili powder
- 2 cups chicken broth
- 4 oz cream cheese
- 1/2 cup sour cream

Instructions:

1. Add chicken, onion, garlic, beans, corn, chilies, spices, and broth to a slow cooker.
2. Cook on low for 6–8 hours or high for 3–4 hours.
3. Shred chicken, stir in cream cheese and sour cream.
4. Cook an additional 15–20 minutes, then serve hot.

Slow-Cooked Sausage and Peppers

Ingredients:

- 1.5 lbs Italian sausage (links or sliced)
- 3 bell peppers, sliced
- 1 large onion, sliced
- 2 cloves garlic, minced
- 1 (14 oz) can crushed tomatoes
- 1 tsp Italian seasoning
- Salt & pepper

Instructions:

1. Place all ingredients in a slow cooker.
2. Cook on low for 6–7 hours or high for 3–4 hours.
3. Serve with hoagie rolls or over rice.

Pork Roast with Apples and Carrots

Ingredients:

- 3–4 lb pork loin roast
- 3 apples, sliced
- 4 carrots, chopped
- 1 onion, chopped
- 1 tsp rosemary
- 1/2 tsp cinnamon
- Salt & pepper
- 1 cup apple cider or broth

Instructions:

1. Place roast in slow cooker. Surround with apples, carrots, and onion.
2. Sprinkle with rosemary, cinnamon, salt, and pepper.
3. Pour in apple cider.
4. Cook on low for 7–8 hours. Slice and serve.

Beef and Potato Stew

Ingredients:

- 2 lbs beef stew meat
- 4 potatoes, chopped
- 3 carrots, chopped
- 1 onion, diced
- 2 cloves garlic, minced
- 3 cups beef broth
- 1 tbsp tomato paste
- 1 tsp thyme, 1 bay leaf
- Salt & pepper

Instructions:

1. Combine all ingredients in a slow cooker.
2. Cook on low for 8 hours or high for 4 hours.
3. Remove bay leaf and serve hot with bread.

Chicken Marsala

Ingredients:

- 2–3 chicken breasts, thinly sliced
- 1/2 cup flour
- 2 tbsp butter
- 1 tbsp olive oil
- 1 cup sliced mushrooms
- 3/4 cup Marsala wine
- 3/4 cup chicken broth
- Salt & pepper
- Fresh parsley

Instructions:

1. Dredge chicken in flour and sear in butter/oil until browned.
2. Remove chicken, add mushrooms, sauté 5 minutes.
3. Add wine and broth, simmer 5 minutes.
4. Return chicken to pan, simmer 10 minutes until sauce thickens.
5. Garnish with parsley.

Slow-Cooked Jambalaya

Ingredients:

- 1 lb andouille sausage, sliced
- 1 lb chicken thighs, cubed
- 1 bell pepper, chopped
- 1 onion, chopped
- 3 cloves garlic, minced
- 1 (14 oz) can diced tomatoes
- 2 tsp Cajun seasoning
- 1 cup chicken broth
- 1 cup rice (add during last hour)

Instructions:

1. Combine all ingredients except rice in slow cooker.
2. Cook on low for 6 hours.
3. Stir in rice and cook 1 more hour or until rice is tender.

Thai Red Curry Chicken

Ingredients:

- 1.5 lbs chicken thighs or breasts, cubed
- 2 tbsp red curry paste
- 1 can (13.5 oz) coconut milk
- 1 tbsp brown sugar
- 1 tbsp fish sauce
- 1 red bell pepper, sliced
- 1 zucchini, sliced
- Fresh basil or cilantro for garnish

Instructions:

1. Add chicken, curry paste, coconut milk, brown sugar, and fish sauce to slow cooker.
2. Cook on low 5–6 hours.
3. Add veggies during the last hour.
4. Garnish and serve with rice.

Slow-Cooked Shepherd's Pie

Ingredients:

- 1.5 lbs ground beef or lamb
- 1 onion, chopped
- 2 cloves garlic, minced
- 2 cups frozen mixed veggies
- 1 tbsp tomato paste
- 1 tsp Worcestershire sauce
- 1/2 cup beef broth
- 4 cups mashed potatoes (spread on top before serving)

Instructions:

1. Brown beef with onion and garlic. Drain fat.
2. Add to slow cooker with veggies, paste, Worcestershire, and broth.
3. Cook on low 6 hours.
4. Spread warm mashed potatoes on top just before serving.

Beef and Vegetable Soup

Ingredients:

- 1.5 lbs stew beef
- 4 cups beef broth
- 2 potatoes, chopped
- 3 carrots, chopped
- 2 celery stalks, sliced
- 1 onion, chopped
- 1 cup green beans
- 1 tsp thyme, 1 bay leaf
- Salt & pepper

Instructions:

1. Add all ingredients to slow cooker.
2. Cook on low for 7–8 hours.
3. Remove bay leaf and serve with bread.

Slow-Cooked Meatloaf

Ingredients:

- 2 lbs ground beef
- 1 onion, finely chopped
- 2 eggs
- 1 cup breadcrumbs
- 1/2 cup milk
- 1/2 cup ketchup + 1/4 cup for topping
- 1 tsp Worcestershire sauce
- Salt & pepper

Instructions:

1. Mix all ingredients except extra ketchup.
2. Form into loaf shape and place in slow cooker on foil or rack.
3. Cook on low 6 hours.
4. Spread ketchup on top in the last 30 minutes.

Chicken and Wild Rice Soup

Ingredients:

- 1 lb boneless, skinless chicken breasts or thighs
- 3/4 cup uncooked wild rice blend
- 3 carrots, chopped
- 3 celery stalks, chopped
- 1 small onion, chopped
- 3 cloves garlic, minced
- 6 cups chicken broth
- 1 tsp thyme
- Salt & pepper
- 1/2 cup heavy cream or half-and-half (optional)

Instructions:

1. Add chicken, rice, carrots, celery, onion, garlic, broth, thyme, salt, and pepper to slow cooker.
2. Cook on low 6–7 hours or high 3–4 hours.
3. Remove chicken, shred, and return to pot.
4. Stir in cream if using and heat through. Serve warm.

Slow-Cooked Baked Ziti

Ingredients:

- 1 lb ziti or penne pasta (slightly undercooked)
- 1 lb Italian sausage or ground beef, cooked and drained
- 3 cups marinara or pasta sauce
- 1 cup ricotta cheese
- 2 cups shredded mozzarella
- 1/2 cup grated Parmesan
- 1 egg
- 1 tsp Italian seasoning

Instructions:

1. Mix ricotta, egg, and Italian seasoning in a bowl.
2. In slow cooker, layer: sauce, pasta, ricotta mixture, meat, mozzarella. Repeat.
3. Top with remaining sauce and mozzarella.
4. Cook on low 3–4 hours. Let sit 10 minutes before serving.

Braised Short Ribs

Ingredients:

- 3–4 lbs beef short ribs
- Salt & pepper
- 2 tbsp olive oil
- 1 onion, chopped
- 2 carrots, chopped
- 2 cloves garlic, minced
- 2 tbsp tomato paste
- 1 cup red wine
- 2 cups beef broth
- 1 tsp thyme, 1 bay leaf

Instructions:

1. Season and sear short ribs until browned, then set aside.
2. Sauté onion, carrots, and garlic. Stir in tomato paste.
3. Deglaze pan with wine, then transfer everything to slow cooker.
4. Add ribs, broth, thyme, and bay leaf.
5. Cook on low 8 hours until tender. Serve with mashed potatoes or polenta.

Chicken Tortilla Soup

Ingredients:

- 1 lb chicken breasts
- 1 can black beans, drained
- 1 cup corn (fresh or frozen)
- 1 (14 oz) can diced tomatoes with green chilies
- 4 cups chicken broth
- 1 small onion, diced
- 2 cloves garlic, minced
- 1 tsp cumin, 1/2 tsp chili powder
- Salt & pepper
- Tortilla strips, sour cream, avocado, cheese (for topping)

Instructions:

1. Add all ingredients (except toppings) to slow cooker.
2. Cook on low 6–7 hours.
3. Shred chicken and return to pot.
4. Top with tortilla strips, cheese, avocado, or sour cream.

Slow-Cooked Goulash

Ingredients:

- 1 lb ground beef or turkey
- 1 onion, chopped
- 2 cloves garlic, minced
- 2 cups uncooked elbow macaroni
- 1 (28 oz) can crushed tomatoes
- 2 cups beef broth
- 1 tsp paprika
- 1 tsp Italian seasoning
- Salt & pepper
- 1 cup shredded cheddar (optional)

Instructions:

1. Brown meat with onion and garlic. Drain.
2. Add to slow cooker with tomatoes, broth, and seasonings.
3. Cook on low 4 hours. Stir in macaroni, cook 30–45 minutes more.
4. Stir in cheese before serving, if desired.

Turkey Chili

Ingredients:

- 1 lb ground turkey
- 1 onion, chopped
- 2 cloves garlic, minced
- 1 (14 oz) can diced tomatoes
- 1 (14 oz) can kidney beans, drained and rinsed
- 1 (14 oz) can black beans, drained and rinsed
- 1 (6 oz) can tomato paste
- 1 cup chicken broth
- 2 tsp chili powder, 1 tsp cumin
- 1/2 tsp smoked paprika
- Salt & pepper
- Optional toppings: sour cream, shredded cheese, cilantro

Instructions:

1. Brown ground turkey with onion and garlic in a pan.
2. Add to slow cooker with all other ingredients.
3. Cook on low for 6–7 hours or high for 3–4 hours.
4. Serve with your choice of toppings.

Slow-Cooked Sausage and Lentils

Ingredients:

- 1 lb sausage (Italian or breakfast sausage), casing removed
- 1 cup dried lentils, rinsed
- 1 onion, chopped
- 2 cloves garlic, minced
- 3 carrots, chopped
- 2 celery stalks, chopped
- 1 (14 oz) can diced tomatoes
- 4 cups chicken or vegetable broth
- 1 tsp thyme, 1 tsp rosemary
- Salt & pepper

Instructions:

1. Brown sausage in a skillet and add to slow cooker.
2. Add lentils, onion, garlic, carrots, celery, tomatoes, broth, and seasonings.
3. Cook on low for 7–8 hours or high for 3–4 hours.
4. Taste and adjust seasoning as needed before serving.

Sweet Potato and Black Bean Stew

Ingredients:

- 2 large sweet potatoes, peeled and diced
- 1 can black beans, drained and rinsed
- 1 onion, chopped
- 2 cloves garlic, minced
- 1 (14 oz) can diced tomatoes
- 1 cup vegetable broth
- 1 tsp cumin, 1/2 tsp paprika
- Salt & pepper
- Optional toppings: avocado, cilantro, lime wedges

Instructions:

1. Add all ingredients to slow cooker.
2. Cook on low for 6–7 hours or high for 3–4 hours.
3. Mash some of the sweet potatoes to thicken the stew, then stir.
4. Serve with toppings if desired.

Slow-Cooked Apple Cinnamon Oatmeal

Ingredients:

- 2 cups rolled oats
- 1 (14 oz) can unsweetened applesauce
- 2 apples, peeled and diced
- 4 cups milk or almond milk
- 1/4 cup brown sugar (optional)
- 1 tsp cinnamon
- Pinch of salt
- Optional toppings: chopped nuts, dried fruit, maple syrup

Instructions:

1. Combine all ingredients in the slow cooker.
2. Cook on low for 6–7 hours or until oatmeal reaches your desired consistency.
3. Stir before serving and add any toppings you like.

Beef and Bean Burritos

Ingredients:

- 1 lb ground beef
- 1 onion, chopped
- 2 cloves garlic, minced
- 1 (14 oz) can black beans, drained and rinsed
- 1 (14 oz) can kidney beans, drained and rinsed
- 1 (14 oz) can diced tomatoes
- 1 tsp cumin, 1/2 tsp chili powder
- Salt & pepper
- 8 large flour tortillas
- 2 cups shredded cheese (cheddar or Mexican blend)
- Optional toppings: sour cream, salsa, guacamole, lettuce

Instructions:

1. Brown ground beef with onion and garlic in a pan.
2. Add beef mixture, beans, tomatoes, cumin, chili powder, salt, and pepper to slow cooker.
3. Cook on low for 6 hours or high for 3 hours.
4. Warm tortillas and spoon beef and bean mixture into each. Top with cheese and desired toppings.

www.ingramcontent.com/pod-product-compliance
Lightning Source LLC
LaVergne TN
LVHW081322060526
838201LV00055B/2414